W9-BDD-534

Science
Vocabulary Readers

Strange Bugs

Justin McCory Martin

SCHOLASTIC INC.

NEW YORK • TORONTO • LONDON • AUCKLAND • SYDNEY
MEXICO CITY • NEW DELHI • HONG KONG • BUENOS AIRES

ISBN-13: 978-0-545-00741-2 / ISBN-10: 0-545-00741-0

Photos Credits:

Cover: © Konrad Wothe/Minden Pictures; title page: © Roy Toft/Getty Images; contents page, from top: © Michael & Patricia Fogden/Minden Pictures, © E.R. Degginger/Animals Animals, © Reinhard H./Peter Arnold Inc., © Mitsuhiko Imamori/Minden Pictures; page 4: © Michael & Patricia Fogden/Minden Pictures; page 5: © Duncan Mcewan/Minden Pictures; page 6: © Mitsuhiko Imamori/Minden Pictures; page 7: © Bill Beatty/Animals Animals; page 8: © E.R. Degginger/Animals Animals; page 9: © Mark Moffett/Minden Pictures; page 10–11: © Mitsuhiko Imamori/Minden Pictures; page 12: © Leroy Simon/Getty Images; page 12, inset: © Charles Melton/Getty Images; page 13: © Barbara Stmadova/Photo Researchers Inc.; page 14: © Reinhard H./Peter Arnold Inc.; page 14, inset: © Stephen Dalton/Minden Pictures; page 15: © Pete Oxford/Getty Images; page 15, inset: © Frans Lanting/Minden Pictures; page 16: © Piotr Naskrecki/Minden Pictures; page 16, inset: © David Tipling/Getty Images; page 17: © Piotr Naskrecki/Minden Pictures; page 17, inset: © Michael W. Richards/Nature Picture Library; page 18: © Frans Lanting/Minden Pictures; page 19: © Mitsuhiko Imamori/ Minden Pictures; page 20: © Michael & Patricia Fogden/Minden Pictures; page 21: © Brian Kenney/OSF/Animals Animals; page 22: © Paul A. Zall/ Getty Images; page 23: © Art Wolf/Getty Images; page 24: © Kevin Schafer/Peter Arnold Inc.; backcover: © Pete Oxford/Getty Images.

Photo research by Dwayne Howard
Design by Holly Grundon

12 11 10 9 8 7 6 5 4 3 2 1   8 9 10 11 12 13/0

Printed in the U.S.A.
First printing, March 2008

Contents

Chapter 1

So Many Strange Bugs

spiky-headed katydid

There are some insects that look very scary.

Only mammals have hair. Some insects have bristles that look like hair.

oak eggar moth

There are some insects that look very hairy.

Fast Fact

This insect's sharp thorn warns other bugs not to eat it.

thorn bug

And there are some insects that look very, very strange!

The two spots on this bug's back are called false eyes. They scare away predators.

eastern-eyed click beetle

In this book, you will meet some of the oddest insects on Earth!

Chapter 2

Very Big Bugs

giant walkingstick

Want to see some really, really big bugs?
Take a look at this giant walkingstick. Put three
crayons in a line. That is how long it is!

Fast Fact

Giant wetas crawl because they are too heavy to jump!

giant weta

Here is another huge bug. It is **related** to the grasshopper, but it is much bigger. Some giant wetas are larger than mice!

Wow! Can you believe the Hercules beetle is this size in real life? Well, it is! Some of them grow to be more than seven inches long.

Hercules beetle

Other Words for Big

- enormous
- huge
- giant
- gigantic
- humongous
- immense
- colossal
- mammoth

Don't worry about those super-sharp horns. This beetle only uses its horns to **joust** with other beetles.

Close Up!

This moth's antennae look like feathers close up.

cecropia moth

Take a look at this lovely moth! It lives in the United States. It is as wide as an open hand when its wings are spread.

This is the wingspan.

Goliath birdwing butterfly

 Fast Fact

The Goliath birdwing is one of the largest butterflies in the world!

Flutter, flutter! You might be surprised if you saw this butterfly in real life. Why? Its **wingspan** is almost one foot long.

Chapter 3

Copycat Bugs

Compare

wasp

wasp beetle

Some insects are strange because they **resemble** other creatures. This bug is called a wasp beetle because it looks like a wasp.

giraffe weevil

Compare

giraffe

This copycat bug is called a giraffe weevil.
It has a very long neck, just like a giraffe.
It likes to eat leaves and seeds.

mole cricket

Compare

mole

This copycat bug is called a mole cricket.
It digs **burrows**, just like a mole. It munches
on worms, grubs, and grass.

peacock katydid

Compare

peacock

This copycat bug is called a peacock katydid. It is beautiful. Do you think it looks like a peacock?

Chapter 4

World's Weirdest Bugs

red stink bug

Meet the stinkbug. But be careful not to frighten it. Why? It **releases** a very bad smell when it is scared.

Dung beetles live for three to five years.

dung beetle

Look at the dung beetle! It is rolling a big ball of **dung**. This insect lays its eggs in dung. It also eats dung. Yuck!

Fast Fact

A scientist who discovers a new insect often chooses the bug's name.

spiny bug

Can you spot the insect in this picture? It is called a spiny bug. Creepy! It really blends in with the plant it is on.

cecropia moth caterpillar

Munch! Munch! This hungry caterpillar may look funny now. But in just a few weeks, it will **transform** into a lovely moth.

treehopper

Wow! There sure are a lot of strange insects in our world. Aren't you glad?

Glossary

bristles (**briss**-uhlz): long, wiry strands that look like hair

burrow (**bur**-oh): a tunnel or hole in the ground used or made by an animal

dung (**dung**): manure; poop

false eyes (**fawlss eyes**): spots on an animal that look like eyes

joust (**joust**): a battle with two lances

related (ri-**lay**-tid): part of the same family

release (ri-**leess**): to free something

resemble (ri-**zem**-buhl): to look like something else

transform (transs-**form**): to make a great change

wingspan (**wing**-span): the distance between the outer tips of the wings of an insect or bird

Comprehension Questions

1. Can you name and describe one big insect?

2. Can you name and describe one copycat insect?

3. Can you name and describe one gross insect?

4. Can you name and describe your favorite strange insect?

Bonus Fast Facts

- There are about 10 quintillion (10,000,000,000,000,000,000) insects in the world.

- Giant wetas have been around for more than 100 million years, since the time of the dinosaurs.

- The ancient Egyptians believed that a giant dung beetle was rolling the sun across the sky.